China

People's Republic

Stephen and Scharlie Platt

www.leveretpublishing.com

China: Imperial past and People's Republic
First published - September 2017
Published by
Leveret Publishing
56 Covent Garden, Cambridge, CB1 2HR, UK

Coloured pottery female figurine Tang AD 618-907

彩绘陶女俑
唐　公元618～907年

ISBN 978-0-9957681-0-6

China
People's Republic

Floral display, Bund Shanghai

China 2012

Heilongjiang
Harbin
Changchun
Jilin
Mongolia
Urumqi
Shenyang
North Korea
Xinjiang
Hohhot
Beijing
South Korea
Yinchuan
China
Xining
Shaanxi
Xi'an
Zhengzhou
Shanghai
Hefei
Tibet
Sichuan
Wuhan
Nepal
Lhasa
Chengdu
Changsha
Fuzhou
Yunnan
Guangdong
Bangladesh
Kunming
Guangxi
Guangzhou
Hong Kong
Myanmar (Burma)
Vietnam
Macau
Laos
Bay of Bengal
Hainan
South China Sea
Thailand

Shanghai

Thursday 1 March

The flight to Shanghai was 10 hours, with a murky descent through cloud, which made Scharlie nervous. After we got through customs a young man offering hotel transport grabbed us. Wendy had said we should pay only half what he asked. He led us to his desk and we asked the girl to ring Wendy who got the price down to 350 CNY, which didn't seem too much as we were whisked off to a sumptuous cream upholstered limo and had a pleasant trip into Shanghai. On the return journey we were in a smoky taxi that cost 200 and both got headaches, so in retrospect it was worth the extra. Funny how on arriving in an unfamiliar country one has this preoccupation with not getting ripped off.

Shanghai is a vast city and we had chosen the Citadenes Hotel in the old city where we thought we would be able to find our way around on foot. We unpacked and had a brief walk around the block to get our bearings before a full breakfast of Chinese style fried egg and interesting vegetables then headed

Scharlie on the Bund Shanghai

back out. It takes resolution to step out of the hotel to explore and we were lost within 10 minutes in spite of our compass. We found a woman who spoke English to ask the whereabouts to the People's Square. She invited us to follow her back the way we had come and it turned out the trick is to stick to the main roads and only go down a side street if it's named and one you recognise.

Friday 2 March

Scharlie spotted a sightseeing bus and we bought a tour of the old city including a visit to the Jade Temple. Our sense of direction was soon scrambled as the bus turned this way and that in a one-way system. It was a circular route and you could get on and off at any of the attractions along the route. We got off at the Bund and walked along the promenade in the cold along with the many Chinese visitors having their photos taken looking across the river to skyscrapers and the Oriental Pearl communications tower in the Pudong New Area. Our guide said we could climb the tower for view or take

Looking across the misty river to the Oriental pearl Tower and Pudong New Area

a boat cruise; choosing what to see is tiring, especially when time is short. But the pall of smoggy mist persisted and we walked the length of the promenade rather than take a boat. We walked as far as the ferry terminal and then back on the other side of the road and went into the Hong Kong and Shanghai Bank building with its fabulous marble foyer. We were enjoying this taste of British imperial past and it was nice to get out of the cold for a minute or two. So a little further on we popped into the Fairmont Peace Hotel, originally the legendary Shanghai Cathay Hotel, a luxurious Art Deco masterpiece built by Victor Sassoon in 1929 with its memories of gaiety and lavish lifestyles. The super courteous hotel staff invited us to visit a small museum of hotel memorabilia and sign the visitors' book. We wrote: A time machine to a gracious past with an uncertain future mushrooming just across the water.

On leaving we were accosted by a couple of friendly girls who asked us to take their photo. They were animated and chatted excitedly in English, saying they were on holiday and questioned us about where we came from. They seemed to want to talk in English. They asked where we'd been and where we wanted to go, saying they went to the places we had on our schedule

Foyer of the Art Deco Fairmont Peace Hotel (Formerly Shanghai Cathay Hotel)

yesterday and they were going to a place where there were Western-style bars and did we want to come. We both felt uneasy, that this was some sales ploy; the girls reluctantly said goodbye.

We dropped off the bus at the Yu Gardens and were immediately tackled again in a similar way by another couple, who wanted us to go to an international tea ceremony, have fun together and enable them to practice their English. Scharlie was strongly tempted and all for going but Steve insisted we stick to the plan and look round the gardens we could see over the fence – contorted trees, lily ponds and pitted rock formations. You enter this part of the city through a monumental arch spanning the road and we quickly found ourselves in a warren of alleys formed by covered stalls selling all manner of goods from food to jewellery and silks. It was a little early in the tourist season, so most of the visitors were Chinese. Scharlie wanted to examine the goods and see prices but even a glance produced an enthusiastic response from the seller. She would have loved to spend more time looking at the silk but didn't dare.

We paid to go into the walled garden, a series of squares leading on from

Yuyuan or Jade Garden

Yuyuan or Jade Garden

each other with numerous small pavilions and bonsai flowering trees some with pink buds just opening. We soon lost our sense of direction, although the garden itself was not very large. In the centre was a large pavilion with a view over the water to an extensive rockery, with a hidden gate guarding a winding path up to a small lookout pavilion. But the rockery and path were closed; perhaps they have to protect it from the pressure of so many visitors or it wouldn't last long.

Jade Temple

At a stall in the road we bought dumplings for lunch and ate them on the bus on the way to the Jade Temple. Scharlie had filled the container so full of gravy that it was hard to manage. She'd also mislaid her earphones and one of Steve's plugged into her left ear kept popping out which meant she got a very disjointed commentary. There was some confusion about where to get off to catch the bus to the Jade Temple and we missed our stop, but our driver rocketed along to the start and we were able to jump onto the next bus as it moved off on the other tour we had paid extra for.

The officials at the Temple examined our papers carefully and explained we could take photographs of everything except the Jade Buddha himself. It was our first temple and therefore most impressive. Scharlie loved the colour combinations of reds and shades of blue, but preferred looking at the buildings from outside where there was space to admire the graceful curve of the roof and its complex ornamentation. The interiors are generally dark and suffocating with incense and overpowering imagery. The Jade Buddha was the exception, housed in a space upstairs with a spacious high ceiling and carved from a single piece of jade. His features were finely carved and his face serene. The

Buddha carved from a single piece of jade

sales technique in the temple complex was more refined than on the street. A young man with excellent English approached Scharlie saying, I suggest you have a look upstairs before you go; there is a laughing Buddha you may find interesting. There was indeed an intricately carved wooden Buddha but also a large number of jade carvings for sale and an informative saleswoman. We didn't buy anything, but the sales lady explained how jade came in a range of shades from near white to dark green and that the craftsman would consider

555 Nanjing West Road

what subject would best bring out the beauty of the stone before he started carving.

On leaving the temple we decided not to wait for the bus but to go to the railway station by taxi to buy our tickets for tomorrow. We had been told by Wendy this was important as our train went from a different station at 8 AM the next day and it would be difficult to buy tickets and from the map it seemed that the ticket office was nearer the Jade Temple than our hotel. At the station we found the information office and got out our passports to buy the tickets but it appeared that the ticket office was some distance down the road and after following a trail of arrows up and down steps and along tunnels we finally managed to buy the tickets and get back to the hotel by taxi well pleased with ourselves.

That evening, after a rest, we ventured forth in search of food and walked down Nanjing East Road and found a place called Home Cooking Restaurant with an interesting menu. The entrance was tatty and it was nearly empty but upstairs there was a spacious and pleasant restaurant and a menu with photographs in English so we managed fine. The food was fantastic and on

Home Cooking Restaurant, Nanjing East Road

our way out we met a Chinese couple who asked us how we found this place. He said he worked for Rolls-Royce in Derby and that colleagues had recommended the restaurant to them and he was impressed we were finding our own way around. We walked back to the East End and bought a cake and gave some change to a grinning father and son begging at the door.

Hangzhou

Saturday 3 March

We got up early because it was a long taxi ride to the railway station, but we made it in good time. The station was very modern and we waited in a large open concourse near the allocated gate, which was manned by a girl in a long red cloak and a cute hat who allowed no one through till 15 minutes before the train was due. We are impressed by the way the Chinese manage vast

Late night shopping, Shanghai

numbers of people. The train was very quiet and comfortable and the journey passed effortlessly. Seats are numbered and comfortable and the movement so silent and steady you are hardly aware you are moving. We were soon in the country and travelling through brick built villages set amongst ordered fields. The land was waterlogged – it had been raining heavily and everywhere looked sodden – they'd had an unusually wet winter and the drainage canals that criss-crossed the fields were full to the brim. On every available patch of land people were growing vegetables all in perfectly straight lines at right angles to the boundary. Even the railway embankment was cultivated where possible.

Wendy was waiting for us and called out Steve and Scharlie excitedly. She was looking beautiful in green wellies, a navy wool coat with a cloak, flowery silk scarf and a pretty peach coloured umbrella. She had finished her Master's degree in Nottingham two years earlier and Steve had supervised her dissertation on the English new towns movement. She was very pleased to see us and took us to have breakfast of churros and porridge in a fast-food joint. It's raining, she said, but don't worry it will be very romantic by the West

Access to the platforms was controlled by girls in red uniforms

Lake.

It was pouring with rain and we took a taxi to the West Lake and walked into the park and wandered around in the rain taking photographs of each other on the bridges and being regaled with romantic legends. The lake was very full and we couldn't see the mountains, but got misty views of the famous Duan Bridge, the lovers bridge. It's so romantic with this mist, said Wendy sitting back in the punt under her pink umbrella. She told us a story about a white snake who fell in love with a young man who had saved her life. Generations later she was reincarnated as a woman and seduced a descendant of the young man by dropping her parasol while crossing the bridge and a young fisher boy had caught it.

We stopped for coffee in a pavilion until Tao arrived and joined us for lunch. He is tall and boyish looking, enthusiastic, friendly and brimming with a youthful self-confidence. They took us to a famous restaurant, which had been recommended by Tao's grandmother and we had a leisurely meal in a very grand room. Wendy and Tao met at Nottingham where she was doing a Masters in architecture and he was studying chemistry. He was brought

Wendy took us for breakfast of churros and porridge

up in England and his father lived in Birmingham and his mother in London where she is an acupuncturist. Tao said his parents were upset when he decided to follow Wendy to China. Wendy had had three job offers and she chose Hangzhou as being a beautiful place to live. Tao had fallen into teaching English to gifted children by making a partnership with a woman who'd been teaching for some years but was badly organised. In a few months his good administration had improved the business, he said, and he had plans for expansion. The main lunch dish was carp from the lake cooked in a sweet and sour sauce and there was an aubergine dish we enjoyed. It was a big occasion for them and they wouldn't let us pay, it's the least we can do, Wendy said.

Afterwards we went walking in the Imperial Gardens in the rain and climbed a steep hill to a tearoom in a pavilion, rather like a relaxed Internet cafe. The path winding through the trees was landscaped in the Chinese style with fantastically shaped limestone rocks. At the top a plaque said that the Emperor liked to walk here to write poetry and contemplate nature. He wrote a poem about how beautiful it was to walk in the mist. For us the garden would have been more beautiful with blue sky and with blossom on the trees; we could

Bridge in West Lake, Hangzhou

Ferryman, Xi Hu, West Lake,Hangzhou

Steve and Scharlie, Xi Hu, West Lake,Hangzhou

West Lake gardens

Lou Wai Lou restaurant, most famous restaurant in Hangzhou, built in 1840

see buds about to burst open on the peach trees lining the lake. Scharlie pointed out mistletoe high on a tree to Wendy and Tao to heighten the romance of the rain.

We walked back towards town to get a taxi and finally managed to find one, despite everyone else trying to get home in the rain. We went to Tao's office, which turned out to be a small rented no-frills room with one or two children bent over books and his partner finishing her lunch. We were warmly received, however, and given a scroll, the calligraphy by Tao's uncle. The aim is to teach English to middle school children. Proper English, as Tao says, as he's lived all his life in England. He's so confident and outgoing he could make a big success of this teaching venture. Tao was catching a plane to Hong Kong to renew his visa and Wendy was relieved when he was safely despatched on the bus; he had so enjoyed chatting in English that he kept putting off his departure. She's happy with Tao and enjoying her job and they plan to marry, despite Tao making her sensitive to what he calls China's Third World hygiene.

Wendy took us for last bite to eat and a walk through a shopping street of traditional shops – the vendors' in traditional costume with a huge range

Imperial gardens, Hangzhou –

of produce on display. Finally she led us to the station and we made our goodbyes. Despite the rain it was a good day and we'd enjoyed wandering and chatting about life in England and China and their hopes and plans for the future.

Beijing

Sunday 4 March

The next morning we had just time to visit the Shanghai Museum. The smoky taxi left us at the National Theatre instead of the museum and fortunately it was only ten minutes away and we recognised it from our bus tour. We had to limit ourselves and decided to see the galleries of ancient Chinese landscape art; calligraphy and porcelain, including some remarkable pottery sculptures from the Tang dynasty of mounted soldiers. The brief time we were there the noise and hurly-burly disappeared and the stress and uncertainties in decision-making fell away and we could immerse ourselves in the painting and ancient

Traditional shops, Hangzhou

Shopping Street, Hangzhou

objects such that the thoughts and intentions of the people who made them seemed immediate and palpable.

Back to the hotel to collect our bags and in a short time we were at the airport and domestic departures with East China Airways with about two hours to spare. During our wait at the departure gate we talked to a nice, intelligent man from Taiwan who owned three factories in Mainland China and was on his way to a trade show in Beijing to show off his bathroom wares. He said he was 60 and liked working but the recession was testing his business and his wife wanted him to retire and take a cruise on a big ship. He admitted this might be an idea, you work all your life so you can have some joy, he said. He also referred to being free in Taiwan, which we found interesting since, as far as commerce was concerned, China seemed very free to us.

It was a short flight to Beijing and we landed in cold sunshine rather than rain. Yingying was waiting for us looking slim and glamorous in high-heeled boots, pale blue cardigan with her nails manicured. Scharlie joked with her about never having seen her look so smart before.

Prof Yin had provided his car and driver for us and we loaded up and were

Shanghai Museum

Polychrome glazed pottery figurine of equestrian. Tang AD 618-907

Pottery duck with low-fired green glaze. Eastern Han AD 25-220

whisked off to the city along the express-way into town. The motorway is lined with closely planted trees all of the same species with white mottled bark like birch. We arrived at the hotel, the Emperor, which Yingying had booked. It turned out we were booked at two hotels and both said they would charge one night penalty so we decided to stay where we were. It cost a bit more than the Kapok Hotel that a colleague had recommended. The only problem was the livid blue decor in the bedroom and the centrally controlled heating. We had to leave the window open and the first night Scharlie was disturbed by traffic noise outside but we got used to the bright decor and found the room comfortable.

Monday 5 March

We were due to meet Prof Yin and I was to give my lecture to the Faculty of Architecture. Yingying collected us in a car with a driver at 9.30 – a civilised hour as we were tired and it allowed time for a great breakfast in the top floor restaurant with a terrace overlooking the Forbidden City. We drove north to the Summer Palace, so called because it was a cool place for the Empress

Yingying takes us to dinner

Dowager Cixi (1835-1908) to go. It's a park set around a vast artificial lake divided by a causeway, with islands and temples. The palace complex dated from much earlier and was begun in 1153 and modified, extended and remodelled many times over its long history. The living quarters are round the perimeter of the lake with covered walkways for exercise and a dock for boats that carried people to the temple and Islands. The lake was frozen still and although the sun was hazy, the prospect was magnificent. There were signs in English and Chinese giving the history of each building and references to an Allied invasion force of Anglo-French who looted and burned the palace in the 19th century during the Opium Wars, Lord Elgin, British High Commissioner for China, ordered the destruction of the old Summer Palace in October 1860 in reprisal for the deaths of two British envoys. This still obviously evokes strong emotions among people in China.

The lake was low and still largely frozen and we were lucky with the weather it was cold and dry and pleasant in the winter sun. It was soon after the Olympics, when air pollution had been reduced by government diktat and high-pressure winter weather meant the air was clear and bright. We walked

Bedroom in Emperor Hotel

Partially frozen Kunming Lake

Entrance to Summer Palace

along the lake shore until we reached the Imperial living quarters. We walked the Long Corridor – an open covered way stretching nearly a kilometre, over another bridge with a romantic story, painted pavilions with dragon roofs and contorted dragon claw trees and beautiful pebble pavements with intricate designs of flowers and animals. Here we saw lots of families out for the day

Contorted tree, Yangyunxuan, Summer Palace

having picnics. Yingying said with some satisfaction that locals had cheap entry for recreation and the same applies to the University campus, which is also free. The Emperor would never be able to imagine this, she said, they sit in the sun all day and play cards and talk or exercise.

We walked onto the artificial Longevity Hill created from the material dug

Yangyunxuan, Summer Palace

from the lake and climbed to its summit and crossed over to the north gate where the driver met us and took us for lunch in the university canteen where we had fish soup. The building has seven floors and Yingying said we were on the one with the best service. Scharlie asked if it was just for postgraduate students and Yingying said all was open to everyone.

The Long Corridor, Qiushuiting, Summer Palace

We drove to the Institute of Urban Planning, which was some way from the University campus. They had just celebrated their 10th anniversary and there were red banner slogans and a wall of photos of members of the Institute. There was also a wall of photos from a photo competition – Prof Yin's hobby is photography. He has, according to Yingying, over 200 cameras. Yingying had

Families visiting Summer Palace

won first prize with a picture of a woman seated in a pool of light in a gallery in Barcelona that we'd seen on her Facebook page. The plan had been to meet Prof Yin with several students for a formal dinner that evening after the lecture but it had been cancelled because Prof Yin had been asked at short notice by the government to go to plan a new city. Yingying then got a

Qingyaoting, pavilion Summer Palace

Example of patterned paving

Curve of Long Corridor, running along lake shore for nearly a kilometre

Leaving by the North gate

Frozen moat of Suzhou Street exit, Summer Palace

telephone call to say that he was hurrying back to the University because his trip had been delayed a day and he would be able to meet Steve briefly after all. The call came to say he had arrived and we were ushered in to his spacious office for the long awaited audience. Prof Yin was slightly shy but smiling and warm, about fifty years old with a short spiky haircut, a big smile, and crinkly eyes. He'd been at an important lunch meeting but was dressed casually in a fleece top and pants and needed to fly off that afternoon to the city he had to plan so could not come to dinner with us this evening. He was most apologetic he couldn't make it and said Yingying should take us instead as his treat. We talked about Cambridge and he said that he and our friend Ying Jin had been students together and Ying was like his brother. His office is most of one floor, has marvellous views on three sides and a place he can sleep and wash. There were brown leather sofas, Artemide lamps and two large Apple computers. They are clearly not short of work or funding and have 800 staff. Yingying says she'd like to help him so maybe she'll work in the Institute full-time when she graduates this summer. She will go and work with him the Saturday after we have left.

Photographic competition at Institute of Urban Planning in which Yingying won first prize

He thanked us for looking after Yingying in England and apologised for having been called away. However important the meeting, I have to go, he said. We talked briefly about Christchurch and he said he had been surprised to hear on BBC that so much was being demolished. Steve had hoped to discuss the reconstruction after the Wenchuan earthquake but Prof Yin didn't bring it up and with only five minutes to go it would have been clumsy of us. He asked after our friend Prof Jin Ying in Cambridge, saying he is my brother. Steve presented him with a bottle of whiskey we had brought specially and Yingying was sent to get us a presentation copy of his book. She then suggested Prof Yin give us a scroll of his own calligraphy and he showed us his brush and his work. Steve asked if he could take a photo and Yingying took one of the three of us. Then it was time to go to the lecture.

There was just time to drive back to the University and set up the lecture. It had been moved from a small classroom to the main auditorium and there was a large poster outside advertising it in the entrance foyer. There were lots of students and the lecture went well. Steve presented his slide lecture in a clear relaxed and humorous way and nothing went wrong with the equipment

Professor Yin Director of Institute of Urban Planning and his office

Scharlie and Yingying grabbing a bite to eat

Steve giving his lecture

except for a few squeaks. Some of the research methods he described will be useful to them and the whole issue of user needs is relevant in China. It went down well, including the music and the colour choice exercises we did at Leveret Croft and a few students asked questions, then it was over and he could relax.

After the lecture we wanted something simple for supper and Scharlie suggested noodles so we went to a popular restaurant called 24/7. This is how the ordinary people live, Yingying said, as we entered a fairly noisy noodle bar. We took a number and waited our turn in what seemed like a dilapidated railway waiting room. Upstairs and Yingying ordered more food than we could eat and watched a young chef swirling pasta to make fresh noodles. Scharlie managed a little better with her chopsticks and Steve coped well with both chopsticks and all the difficult dishes. Scharlie had to stick mainly to vegetables but even this was difficult as they come in strange guises and flavours. The worst was lotus root coated in sugar, but she liked the fresh lotus root, bamboo shoots, rice fried or steamed, been curd and aubergine.

Steve wanted to go for a drink to celebrate his lecture so we were driven

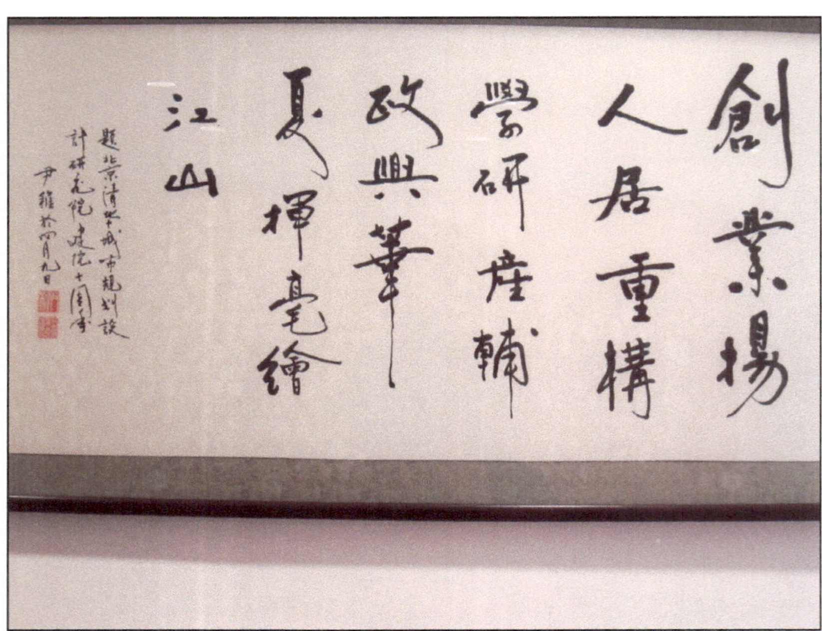

Example of calligraphy in Institute of Planning foyer

to the 'village', a swanky area in the centre and found a bar Yingying had been to before. It's modern, all glass and bright colours, next to an area where Europeans live, and features adventurous high quality architecture. It's a popular place for young people to come and look at fashion. China is welcoming the big brands and there were huge adverts for Burberry and Adidas. Steve wanted beer, which the waitress seemed to find odd since everyone else was drinking cocktails. The interior design was impressive – a glass and wood screen decorated with Chinese traditional symbols and objects, like an apothecary's medicine cabinet. It would be good for your economy, Yingying said, to give Chinese tourists one week shopping visas; it's strange that you are trying to keep is out.

Tuesday 6 March

The next day the driver came for as early to take us to the Great Wall. We'd decided to go to Muntanye, because our guide described it as mountainous with fewer tourists. We had an argument about which cable car to take and then, when we reached the top Steve wanted to go right to what looked

Bar screen in the Village, a swanky new shopping centre

the most exciting part of the wall with snow and less people and Scharlie wanted to go left into the sun. Steve got his way and we set off. It was steep and slippery in parts but we made it as far as the watchtower where two walls crossed and the continuation was prohibited as the wall unrepaired and crumbling. We went a little way to get a view into Mongolia and then turned back. We chatted to a vendor selling postcards who said he lived in the village we could see to the north. He pointed out the track and said it was

Muntanye section of the Great Wall

Scharlie climbing icy section of Great Wall

Sunnier end of the wall

in Mongolia and we could go there if we wanted to. This is Chinese Mongolia rather than the country.

We walked back to the ski lift station and then on the other way as far as the big cable car a couple of miles further on. We stopped at a watchtower and sat in the sun on the steps and had our lunch in the warm sunshine. At the cable car we turned back and walked back to the lowest point on the wall and took a broad stone path leading through woodland down to the village where we had left the car and driver.

At the bottom of the hill we had to battle through a phalanx of women selling all kinds of tat from pandas to brightly coloured dressing gowns. Steve managed to get through the turnstile, having agreed we wouldn't buy anything, when Scharlie called. She had been collared by woman selling pandas and she finally negotiated to buy six for too much money and then had a fight to get her change back – the woman trying to sell her a big Panda. Scharlie was pleased she got presents for all her grandchildren.

We picked up Yingying and walked around the university campus admiring the library and Aula Magna, built with American money in about 1910 in the style of Columbia University, and then the lake, garden and pavilion in the Chinese style. The campus is huge, spacious and well planned and even though everything was brown – the snow had only just recently melted – it was a

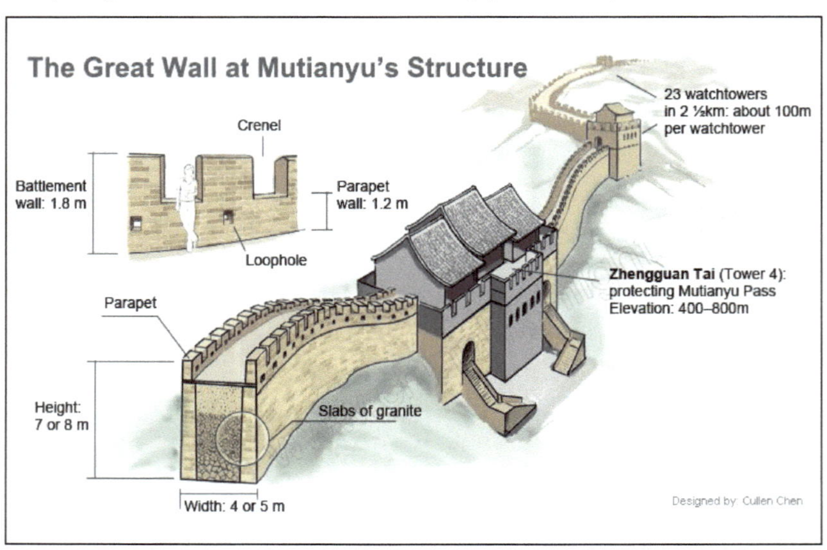

Walking down winding path through woods back to the car

Tsinghua University old library building

Tsinghua University old library

bright sunny day and everything looked beautiful.

We drove to the Lama Temple that Yingying wanted us to see, arriving at four just before it closed and managed to buy tickets. We wandered through the courtyards and temple buildings, arranged symmetrically rather like the palaces with similar rules, colour palette and bronze sculptures. The temple has been here about 200 years and I was confused about the status of the Dalai Lama. This is clearly China's Dalai Lama and Yingying was a bit vague about the status of the Lamasery and how it related to Tibet, saying that China had liberated Tibet from the feudal oppression of the Dalai Lama. Steve sat in the sun resting and missed seeing a final temple with an 18m Buddha carved from a single trunk of sandalwood.

We had dinner that night in a hotpot restaurant and although it was very good and the service excellent from a sweet young waiter we weren't very hungry.

Tsinghua University park

Lama Temple

Hot-pot restaurant and our last meal with Yingying

Wednesday 7 March

The next morning we had to ourselves to go round the Forbidden City. We did our homework and despite Yingying and the hotel staff saying we should get a taxi we decided to walk. Scharlie wasn't that keen but it was warm and pleasant in the sun and by the time we reached the moat around the palace after only five minutes walk she had changed her mind. We strolled

Young man making longevity noodles, hotpot restaurant

through the city on its central axis from south to north, returned by the West Wing, then crossed to the Treasury and the inner palace and had lunch on a bench facing the Dragon Wall of blue and yellow ceramic friezes. A huge number of precious objects are still housed in the city and all the palaces still have the furniture and fittings as they were when the last Emperor Puyi was overthrown in 1924, but they are dusty, unloved and badly in need of polish. Yet it is remarkable and admirable that the new regime has kept it all intact and is maintaining the buildings. It was fascinating to see the faces of the Chinese tourists, many in traditional ethnic costume from far-flung parts of the 'empire', talking in different tongues. They pushed and jostled in a way we would find rude or aggressive in England, but seemed intimate and friendly in China; their faces pressed to the glass windows, to catch glimpses of Imperial life, they seemed particularly intrigued by the bed chambers and marital jewels in the Treasury. Everyone ignored us, the two Western tourists in a sea of Chinese, yet this all changed abruptly. I had spotted a granite block about a metre high, worn smooth by many hands and decided to climb on it to take a photo. I had nearly made it when my foot slipped and I fell backwards heavily and landed like an upside down turtle. Suddenly I was surrounded by solicitous

Moat around the Forbidden City

Many parties of Chinese tourists

Fascination with Imperial bed-chambers

Tourists in ethnic dress at Forbidden City

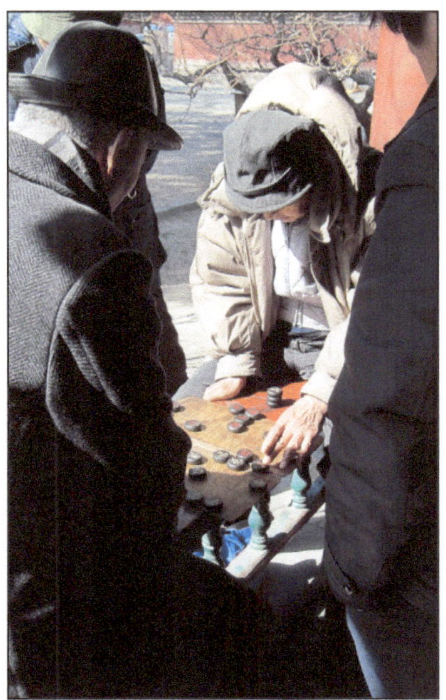

Scenes from the Forbidden City

Chinese kindly asking me, in English, if I was all right and helping me to my feet.

Before leaving we visited the 1910 telephone exchange and learned about the various eunuchs; satraps and functionaries that had wanted to introduce Western ideas. The Dowager Empress Cixi, who featured largely since she reigned for 60 years, was reputed to have drowned the concubine Wu who had supported the Emperor's efforts to Westernise.

That afternoon we were picked up from the hotel and taken to the Temple of Heaven, one of the very few traditional buildings with a round form. We walked along the gently sloping causeway in the opposite direction to the way the Emperor would enter and Steve had his photo taken standing on the stone representing the centre of heaven surrounded by rings of 9, 18 and 81 stones representing eternity and longevity.

Qing Dynasty Cixi Imperial Dowager Empress of China

That night we had the banquet with three other students in the VIP room of a swanky restaurant with a round table. I mischievously sat Scharlie at the head of the table, which discomfited the waiter; this is where Prof Yin would have sat. We had sea cucumber porridge, pungent cress, prawns, raw salmon and a skate. We enjoyed the evening. The students were clever and keen. Steve asked why they wanted to do a Ph.D. and they gave good answers – one said

Hall of Prayer for Good Harvests largest building in the Temple of Heaven where the Emperor prayed for good harvests.

Heart of Heaven or the Supreme Yang, where the Emperor prayed for favourable weather

they wanted to discover something amazing and Yingying said she wanted to find out about herself. Steve said he'd done a PhD because he was invited to, and that lots of things in his life had happened that way. We got to bed early and next morning set off home.

Thursday 8 March

We started two hours late due to late arrival from England after technical problems and were in the very back tail of the plane where there were two seats instead of three and there was more room. There were only 50 passengers booked so there was room to move about and spread ourselves or even lie down on four seats. The take-off was into severe wind and the climb felt as if we were inside a fish swishing its tail. We hoped they'd sorted out the technical problems. Now we are above the clouds at 10,000 feet and following the flight on the screen with a fabulous view over Mongolia and Siberia.

Dinner with Yingying and three prospective doctoral students

Airport departure

Over Siberia

www.ingramcontent.com/pod-product-compliance
Lightning Source LLC
LaVergne TN
LVHW052258100826
845147LV00001B/83

* 9 7 8 1 9 1 2 4 6 0 1 0 6 *